BIOGRAPHIES

GEORGE WASHINGTON
FARMER, SOLDIER, PRESIDENT

Written by Pamela Hill Nettleton
Illustrated by Jeff Yesh

Special thanks to our advisers for their expertise:
Gregory L. Kaster, Ph.D., Chair, Department of History
Gustavus Adolphus College, St. Peter, Minnesota
Susan Kesselring, M.A., Literacy Educator
Rosemount–Apple Valley–Eagan (Minnesota) School District

PICTURE WINDOW BOOKS
MINNEAPOLIS, MINNESOTA

Managing Editor: Bob Temple
Creative Director: Terri Foley
Editor: Peggy Henrikson
Editorial Adviser: Andrea Cascardi
Copy Editor: Laurie Kahn
Prototype: Ann Berge
Page production: The Design Lab
The illustrations in this book were rendered digitally.

PICTURE WINDOW BOOKS
5115 Excelsior Boulevard
Suite 232
Minneapolis, MN 55416
1-877-845-8392
www.picturewindowbooks.com

Printed in the United States of America.

Library of Congress Cataloging-in-Publication Data
Nettleton, Pamela Hill.
George Washington : farmer, soldier, president /
written by Pamela Hill Nettleton ; illustrated by Jeff Yesh.
p. cm. – (Biographies)
Summary: A brief biography that highlights some important
events in the life of the man who was the first President of the
United States.
Includes bibliographical references (p.) and index.
ISBN 1-4048-0184-7
1. Washington, George, 1732–1799–Juvenile literature.
2. Presidents–United States–Biography–Juvenile literature.
[1. Washington, George, 1732–1799. 2. Presidents.]
I. Yesh, Jeff, 1971– ill. II. Title.
E312.66 .N48 2003
973.4′1′092–dc21   2003004119

George Washington became the first president of a new country—the United States of America. He is best known for this role, but George did many jobs well. He owned a big, successful farm. He was a great soldier. Before he became president, he was the commander in chief of the first American army.

Many years later, people still honor George Washington as a great leader. This is his story.

The world was very different when George Washington was born than it is today. America was not even its own country. It was made up of 13 colonies that belonged to England. Virginia was one of those colonies.

George was born in Virginia in 1732. His father was a farmer. No one guessed that George would become one of the most famous people in history.

When George was 11, his father died. George's older half brother, Lawrence, was like a father to him.

George went to school until he was 14 or 15. He was very smart, and he kept on learning new things. When he was 16, George became a surveyor, mapping land in the Virginia wilderness.

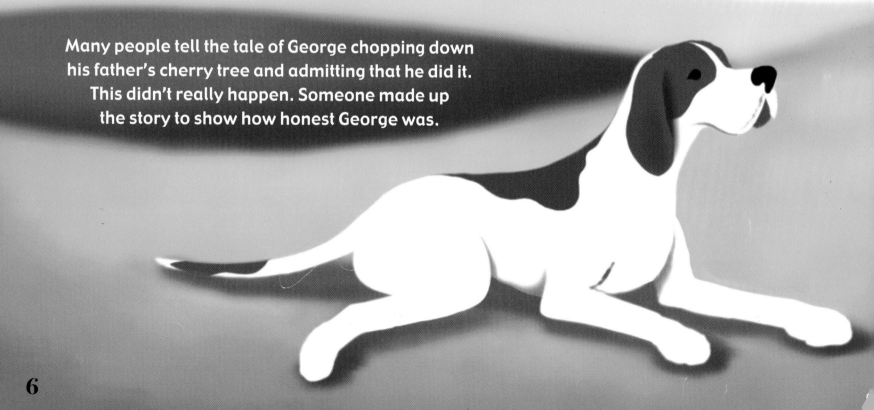

Many people tell the tale of George chopping down his father's cherry tree and admitting that he did it. This didn't really happen. Someone made up the story to show how honest George was.

When George was in his 20s, he fought in the French and Indian War. He led English soldiers and colonists against the French to win land.

One of George's favorite horses was named Blueskin, and one of his dogs was named Sweetlips.

8

George learned how to fight.
He also learned how to work
with people. He was a good leader,
and the army promoted him.

After the war, George went home to his big farm called Mount Vernon. He married Martha Custis and became a stepfather to her two children.

George and the colonists bought many things from England that they couldn't get in America. The king of England made them pay taxes on things such as tea and stamps.

By the time he was 41, George owned about 45,000 acres (18,264 hectares) of land. He raised tobacco, wheat, oats, peaches, and apples.

The colonists were angry and asked the king to stop the taxes. He said no. George and the colonists decided to fight back.

The king sent soldiers to fight the colonists. The colonists asked George to lead the new American army against the English. This was the Revolutionary War.

One thing the colonists did to fight back was to dump a shipload of tea into Boston Harbor. This was the Boston Tea Party.

It was hard to fight the war. George and his soldiers were tired and cold. They often ran out of supplies.

George gave some of his own money to help the soldiers. They lost many battles, but George never gave up.

General Washington taught his soldiers to follow rules. They could not have won the war without his leadership.

Finally, the colonists won the war. Some of the soldiers asked George to be their king.

He did not want to be king. He did not even want to be president, but the new country needed a leader.

The people thought George was a hero, but he did not brag about himself. This made them like him even more.

George helped put together the new government. The colonies became states. The people elected George the first president of the United States.

It was not easy being the president of a new country. The states did not know how to work together.

George led the states well and made the country stronger.

George helped make the rules that other presidents after him would follow. He was president for eight years.

Then George went home to take care of his farm. He died two years later. George Washington is remembered for being brave and wise. He is called the Father of His Country.

The Washington Monument was built
in Washington, D.C., to honor George.
It was completed in 1884 and rises
550 feet (168 meters) into the air.
This is about as high as
a 55-story building!

THE LIFE OF GEORGE WASHINGTON

1732   Born in Virginia on February 11

1748   Became a land surveyor, mapping land, when he was 16

1754–1758   Fought in the French and Indian War

1759   Married Martha Dandridge Custis

1775   Became commander in chief of the Continental Army

1781   Won the battle at Yorktown, Virginia, ending the Revolutionary War

1787–1788   Elected president of the Constitutional Convention and signed the new Constitution of the United States

1789   Elected the first president of the United States at age 57. George was president until 1797.

1799   Died at Mount Vernon, Virginia, on December 14 at age 67

Did You Know?

- George Washington was born on February 11, 1732. When George was 19 years old, England changed the calendar and added 11 days to it. This made George's birthday February 22.

- George wore false teeth made out of human teeth, cow's teeth, elephant tusk, and metal. It hurt to wear them. Maybe that is why we never see a painting of him smiling!

- It was popular for men to wear white wigs in George's day, but George did not wear one. He powdered his hair and tied it in back.

- When he was president, George and his wife, Martha, lived in Philadelphia and New York. George helped plan Washington, D.C., but it was not yet the nation's capital. George is the only U.S. president who never lived in the White House.

- George's face is carved into a mountain called Mount Rushmore in South Dakota. The faces of U.S. presidents Thomas Jefferson, Abraham Lincoln, and Theodore Roosevelt also are carved into Mount Rushmore.

- George's face is on U.S. quarters and one-dollar bills. Many things have been named after George Washington, too: the nation's capital, a state, a mountain, universities, streets, and buildings.

Glossary

colonist (KOL-uh-nist)—someone living in a colony or a land that is newly settled

colony (KOL-uh-nee)—a group of people living in a new land who still are ruled by the country from which they came. Before the Revolutionary War, the United States was 13 colonies ruled by England.

constitution (kon-stuh-TOO-shuhn)—the written ideas and laws upon which a government is based

Constitutional Convention (kon-stuh-TOO-shuh-nuhl kuhn-VEN-shuhn)—the meetings during which a group of people wrote the Constitution of the United States

government (GUHV-urn-muhnt)—the group of people who make laws, rules, and decisions for a country or state

half brother (HAF BRUHTH-ur)—a boy or man who has one of the same parents as another person

stepfather (STEP-fah-thur)—a man who marries someone's mother after the death or divorce of the person's father

tax (TAKS)—money that people or businesses must give to the government to pay for what the government does

TO LEARN MORE

At the Library

Adler, David A. *A Picture Book of George Washington.* New York: Holiday House, 1989.

Pingry, Patricia A. *Meet George Washington.* Nashville, Tenn.: Ideals Children's Books, 2001.

Schaefer, Lola M. *George Washington.* Mankato, Minn.: Pebble Books/Capstone Press, 1999.

Thoennes Keller, Kristin. *George Washington.* Mankato, Minn.: Bridgestone Books, 2002.

Woods, Andrew. *Young George Washington: America's First President.* Mahwah, N.J.: Troll Associates, 1992.

On the Web

THE WHITE HOUSE: GEORGE WASHINGTON

For a brief biography of George Washington

http://www.whitehouse.gov/history/presidents/gw1.html

SMITHSONIAN NATIONAL PORTRAIT GALLERY: GEORGE WASHINGTON, A NATIONAL TREASURE

For a "Portrait for Kids" mystery and a teacher's guide

http://www.georgewashington.si.edu/kids/index.html

Fact Hound

Fact Hound offers a safe, fun way to find Web sites related to this book. All of the sites on Fact Hound have been researched by our staff.

http://www.facthound.com

1. Visit the Fact Hound home page.
2. Enter a search word related to this book, or type in this special code: 1404801847.
3. Click on the FETCH IT button.

Your trusty Fact Hound will fetch the best sites for you!

On a Trip

MOUNT VERNON

Eight miles south of Alexandria, Virginia

(703) 780-2000 for visitor information

http://www.mountvernon.org/visit

For directions, map, hours, programs, and tours

THE WASHINGTON MONUMENT

Washington, D.C.

(202) 426-6841 for visitor information

http://www.nps.gov/wamo

For a printable travel guide

INDEX